A Congress WBN Publication

Produced By:

 and

DISCOVERING God TOGETHER

Discovery Workbook #1

THIS BOOK BELONGS TO:
_____

About the WE MAGNIFY YOU Discovery Workbook Series

Our families are at the core of our Kingdom Communities. The WE MAGNIFY YOU album provides us with a wonderful opportunity to develop and strengthen the expression of worship in our homes.

Each We Magnify You Discovery Workbook has been designed for parents, guardians, teachers and children to experience and explore the songs together.

Discover new sight of what it means to magnify, exalt and praise our God. Together, our families will develop a deeper and stronger understanding of who God is, releasing a whole-hearted expression of worship unto Him.

For each song on the WE MAGNIFY YOU album, we have a Workbook with the lyrics and specially created activities.

Enjoy taking time together to consider what the lyrics mean. Explore scripture verses that tell us more about each song. Engage in fun activities, including word puzzles and coloring games.

Through it all we can together gain a deeper understanding of how the words we sing reflect the lives we must live, as we align ourselves to God.

Now that is a beautiful thing!

Guidance for Parents

The WE MAGNIFY YOU worship album from Congress MusicFactory contains prayers and songs from Dr. Woodroffe and saints from Elijah Centre and Kingdom Communities across Congress WBN.

WE MAGNIFY YOU is a powerful expression of worship and praise to our Lord. Each workbook in the We Magnify You Discovery Series explores the lyrics of the songs, sharing explanations, key scriptures and fun activities.

These resources will help us to align our lives, our families and our communities to the words that we lift unto God.

YOU ALONE

LYRICS

With all of my heart
I worship You
In all of my life
I honor You

Master of my life
I give my all
I give my praise to You alone

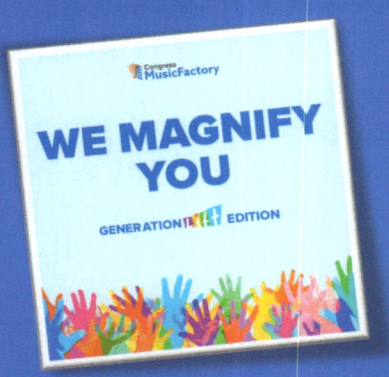

To You alone
You alone
I give my praise to You alone
You alone
You alone
I give my praise to You alone

A CLOSER LOOK

With all of my heart I worship You

When we say the words, **"With all of my heart I worship You,"** we are saying to God, "Here is my whole heart, I give it all to You, I hold nothing back."

So when we worship, we do it with all our might, all our strength and all our heart.

When we worship, we are focusing on God, and telling Him how happy we are to have Him close to us.

Read Psalm 86:10 - 12 to remind yourself to worship God with a whole heart.

WE MAGNIFY YOU Discovery Workbook Series

Choose the correct puzzle piece to complete the heart and color it in.

Remember—we worship God with our **whole heart**!

BOOK 1: You Alone

In all of my life I honor You means that whatever we are doing, we are representing God. In all our thoughts, words and actions, we are showing others exactly what He is like.

When we follow God's ways (for example, by loving others), we are honoring Him. What other kinds of behavior are honoring to God?

Let's remember that every time we sing the line, **"In all my life I honor You,"** we are transforming to become just like Him.

Master of my life I give my all

God is the **Master of our lives**. A master is someone who is in charge of someone else.

This is the reason we give Him our all - never half-hearted.

God is our master so we must always do our very best for Him in everything that we do.

Psalm 16:2
I said to the Lord, "You are my Master! Every good thing I have comes from you."

Activity Time

Can you unscramble the following words found in the lyrics of the song?

Talk to someone about what these words mean!

HREAT	_ _ _ _ _
PROSWHI	_ _ _ _ _ _ _
OORHN	_ _ _ _ _
SRMETA	_ _ _ _ _ _
RASPEI	_ _ _ _ _ _
NALEO	_ _ _ _ _

ANSWER: HEART, WORSHIP, HONOR, MASTER, PRAISE, ALONE

BOOK 1: You Alone

I give my praise to You alone

Only God deserves our praise. Praising Him means that we're telling Him that He is awesome, amazing and incredible - the best! When we give something to one person alone, it means we don't share it with anyone else.

God wants us to **give our praise to Him alone**. There may be other things in life that we value—but in worship, we are giving all our praise to our God!

Draw or write the things you love, putting them in their rightful place on the podium—under God.

God is in His right place, above everything, He is first—He is the best!

BOOK 1: You Alone

A CLOSER LOOK

To You Alone, To You Alone

Sometimes we say something lots of times to help our brain remember it.

Think about when you have to learn new words to spell. We repeat them over and over. It's the same when we are praising God - we repeat our words of worship, so that it is written on our hearts.

To You alone God, to You alone - nothing else will get in the way of my worship to You, because I love You, Lord.

Use the following letters to find out what Levi is saying:

USAOENOIPTEL YIOAYEMRGVI

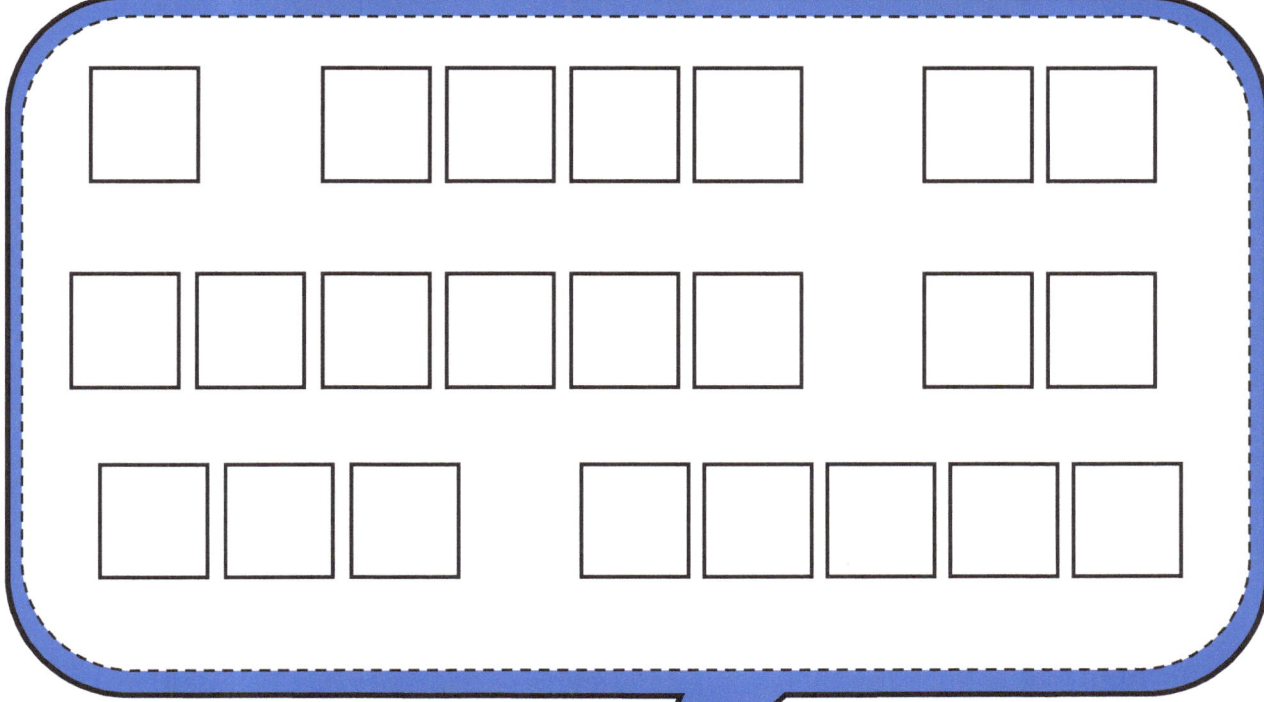

ANSWER: I GIVE MY PRAISE TO YOU ALONE

BOOK 1: You Alone

We are telling God that we praise Him alone. We thank God all the time because He is great.

When we worship God and tell Him **"I give my praise to You alone,"** we are saying that every day, on our best days and in difficult times, we will always praise Him!

Psalm 75:1 says: We proclaim how great you are and tell of the wonderful things you have done.

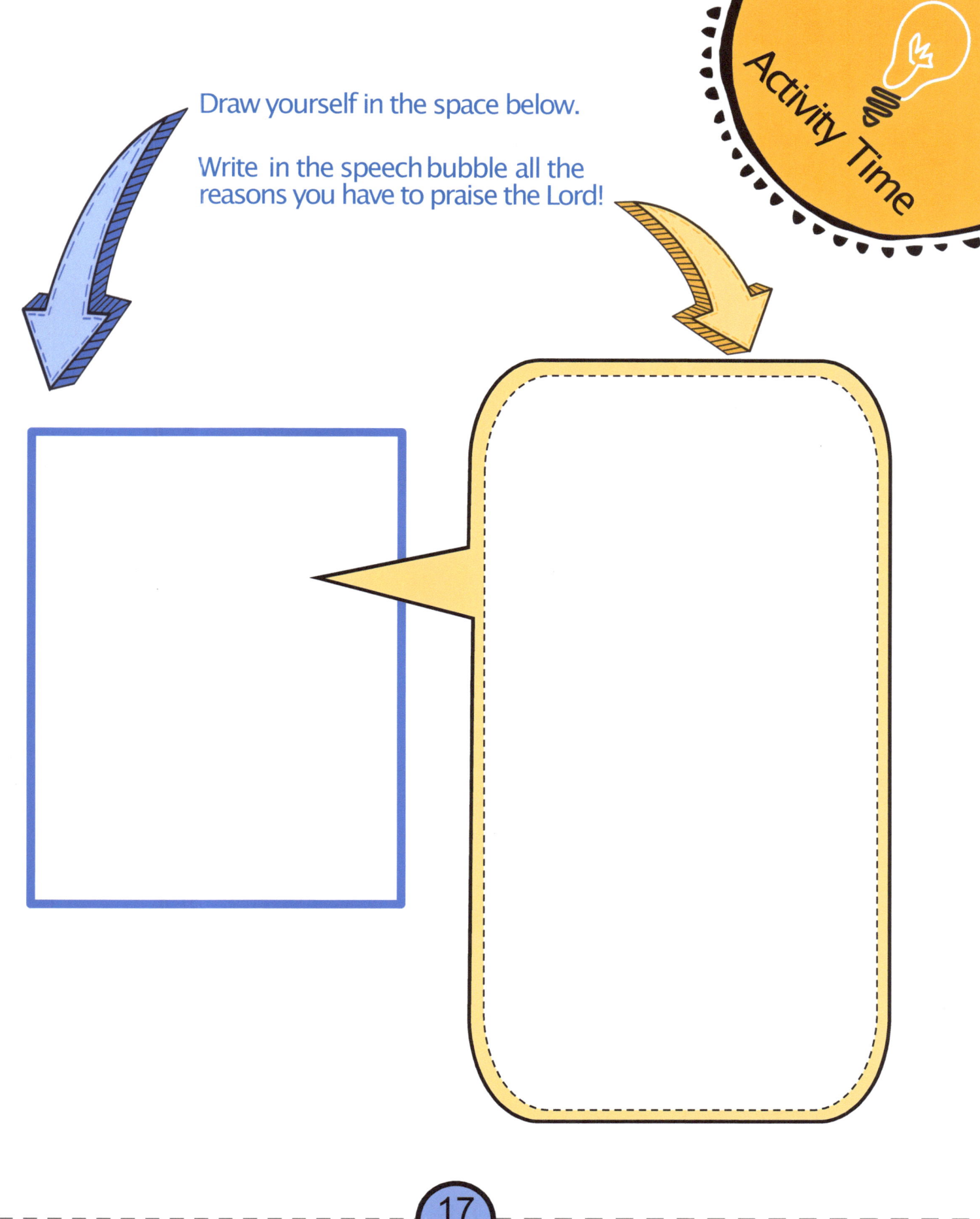

We finish by telling Him once again, and we sing it loudly and joyfully so that everyone can hear the words that are coming from our hearts.

All my praise is going to You, God. No one or nothing else deserves this honor!

Look into the hearts to search for the words from the song.

Understanding these words will help you worship God.

```
A S D E T Y U B G I V E P K
L N U W Q D T X O P C N I W
L B S H D E G H R Y O A P L
O T Z L I F E S T O E G F C
H E A N M A K H O U A L O E
W O R T C H D A R E T S A M
A L O P W O E R S A K P O V
W L K E T Y U A N I U Y R H
M O R I E S I A R P L K U N
W O S H Q B A S M T R E O V
W E R H T Y U I D L E P N P
C V F E I U F D G O V A O K
K L R D S P I O L P M I H U
G I A L O N E V E H T F W E
```

ALL
HEART

HONOR
ALONE

PRAISE
YOU

MASTER
LIFE

WORSHIP
GIVE

BOOK 1: You Alone

> Take some time to reflect on this song. Here's some space to write down your thoughts.

MY JOURNAL

www.ingramcontent.com/pod-product-compliance
Lightning Source LLC
Chambersburg PA
CBHW040326100526
44584CB00002BA/259